FLYING WAS MY DESTINY

THE TRUE FLYING ADVENTURES OF HANS VANDERVLUGT

AS TOLD TO
MARION REAMY

WestBow
PRESS
A DIVISION OF THOMAS NELSON

WestBow Press books may be ordered through booksellers or by contacting:

WestBow Press
A Division of Thomas Nelson
1663 Liberty Drive
Bloomington, IN 47403
www.westbowpress.com
1-(866) 928-1240

Because of the dynamic nature of the Internet, any web addresses or links contained in this book may have changed since publication and may no longer be valid. The views expressed in this work are solely those of the author and do not necessarily reflect the views of the publisher, and the publisher hereby disclaims any responsibility for them.

Any people depicted in stock imagery provided by Thinkstock are models, and such images are being used for illustrative purposes only.

Certain stock imagery © Thinkstock.

ISBN: 978-1-4497-6736-5 (sc)
ISBN: 978-1-4497-6737-2 (e)

Library of Congress Control Number: 2012917051

Printed in the United States of America

WestBow Press rev. date: 10/12/2012

For Milo, my darling husband,

My computer 'guy' who

deserves all the credit for

getting this book ready

for publication

"I have learned that
it is not the mountains
that makes destiny,
but the grains of sand
and the little pebbles."

-B. Traven

PREFACE

On February 19th, 2012 there was an accident at the Yampa Valley Regional Airport in Colorado. A winter storm had shrouded the airport with deep snow. A twin engine Cessna 414A was approaching the airport and was preparing to land and then unexpectedly crashed about 95 yards from the runway. The experienced pilot, Hans Vandervlugt and a passenger were killed on impact. The four other passengers were severely injured and were hospitalized. The cause of the accident is unknown at this time and is under investigation by the NTSB and the FAA.

Hans and his wife Ruth were dear friends of mine and when I heard about the accident my thoughts went back to years ago when Hans had taped many stories for me about his flying adventures. The transcribed pages lay on a shelf waiting to be published. The stories covered a lifetime of flying and accomplishments. These flights were across barren and lonely deserts and oceans that had little or no communications. He flew to countries where it was dangerous to land and refuel. Hans logged more than 70,000 hours flying time during those years. He is really telling his own story as he lived it, because all of the words in the text were transcribed directly from the tapes.

Words cannot express how sorry we are for these families that have lost their loved ones and our thoughts and prayers go to all those who endured this terrible loss.

CONTENTS

LIST OF ILLUSTRATIONS

I

THE JAW BREAKER - 1960

Your first impression of Hans is that you want to find out more about him because of his enthusiasm for flying and the sincere interest he has in his friends. Hans and his wife, Ruth run Vanair Services at Refugio (Rah-fear-e-o) which is out on the vast sun baked lands of South Central Texas. Hans's life is all about flying both in the present and in the stories from his past. You are curious about the enormous scar that runs across the width of his forehead and along the hairline. He laughed when I inquired about it and his hand smoothed the thick dark hair away from his forehead as he lightly touched the scar. His speech changed then from his rapid-fire way of talking and he paused a minute and then began this breathtaking account of what happened to him when he was flying in Canada.

"During the winter of 1960 I was living in Canada in a place called Athabasca in north Central Alberta, it was very remote and about one hundred miles north of Edmonton. I was flying for a construction company that was doing oil field construction work in the bush country and I was flying a Piper Super Cub for survey work and hauling parts for the different bulldozers, caterpillars, and trucks and also supporting the different drilling companies that we also were working for. One of the oil rigs had finished drilling in their location and was ready to move over to their next site and they had not been able to survey their next location because the weather had been terrible. They had been looking for an old survey line that had been cut through the bush many years ago. The drilling crew was worried and anxious with the cost of just sitting around idle waiting for the weather to clear."

Here Hans fairly bounced around the room with his eyes gleaming with excitement. He said, "You know who volunteered to go look for that base line? Yes, of course it was me and I flew a short test hop right that day around the area and I decided even though the ceiling was only 200 feet that I would give it a try."

"I found the location and then found the survey base line and then the ceiling got right down to the ground. The Super Cub having no radio communications and not having any instruments for instrument flying put my buns in a perilous spot. I was flying in ice fog just at the tree tops and even then couldn't see the trees and had the airplane slowed down and all I could see were the tree trunks. I had been following a particular cut line in the bush which showed up like a white pencil line against the dark trees. I also knew where the line was going and I knew it would end up at a lake or near the lake and my plan was to land on that frozen lake."

"I think right then my luck ran out. I had reached the lake sooner than I had anticipated and as the dark of the trees disappeared my thought was that I had inadvertently been flying too high. I nosed the airplane down just slightly to line up my landing and then I made contact with the ground. The airplane winged down and one wing hit and one ski hit. When I came to, I found that I was outside of the airplane on my knees leaning over the wing. I had either crawled out or was thrown out and I remember seeing the registration of the airplane and realizing that it was me that had the accident. I tried to open my mouth and couldn't do it and yet could feel cold air rushing into my throat. Some of my lower teeth were stuck tight in the roof of my mouth and there was a big hole or gash in my jaw right where I had hit the crossbar. This bar is above the instrument panel in a Super Cub. I had no pain and I think what happened was that I had been knocked out and had lost a great amount of blood."

"As I lay across the wing I could see the blood running down into the snow. It was running into my eyes and in my mouth. One of the side plates of the airplane must have come in and had scraped the skin off my forehead peeling it back right down to the bone and just went right on back and peeled off the top of my head as if I had been scalped. I reasoned that I had to do something quickly and thought of the plastic bag used for hauling frozen fish that was in the plane. I wrapped the plastic around my head tightly to keep the blood from running in my eyes and then drew the parka hood of my eider-down filled jacket over that and cinched the string tight."

"I took my sleeping bag from the plane and crawled across the snow covered lake. The snow was deep on the lake and I didn't know if I could make it but I managed to get onto the shore and underneath some spruce trees. The lower boughs were thick and I put the sleeping bag there and crawled into it. Time stood still for me then as I lay suspended in this icy cocoon and I didn't think there was any hope of someone finding me in this desolate place. Later I was told I laid there for three days."

"Then I heard something! A faint sound was coming from across the lake and the sound was like dogs yipping. It was an Indian trapper with his dog sled and the team were making a big sweep across the lake towards me. The trapper was hollering and cussing the dogs and trying to get them turned back, but his lead dog must have smelled me and was leading the team over to me. They were coming closer and closer and suddenly that lead dog came crashing through the snow and branches dragging the sled and driver right to me. Hallelujah! I was saved."

"The trapper threw everything out of his sled and loaded me onto it and took off for the nearest settlement and from there they radioed for help to a drilling site but the weather was fearsome and nobody was flying. Finally, they dozed a trail through the snow and brought out a pickup truck. I really wasn't aware of all of this going on around me and apparently the loss of blood and plus the temperature which had dropped down to 40 below zero all combined to keep infection from getting started in my deep wounds. Now, I shudder to think about the piece of plastic with the fish slime in it that I wrapped around my head."

"There was an ambulance with a doctor waiting at the oil rig and right on the spot I got a blood transfusion and that's when the pain started. From there I was taken to Edmonton University Hospital where I went into the operating room and it took seven hours to put my head back together. Now, I found out how extensive my injuries were and that my jaw was broken in five places and part of my jaw was stuck in the roof of my mouth. One side of my jaw was not damaged so they made a mold of that side and then they would use it as a model for the injured side. The jaw was so painful when they moved the pieces around to put the bones back in place and what they did is they pushed all the pieces together and a pin was put in place to hold it all together. I had only a few teeth left on the bottom row and later after everything was healed a plate was made. The nerves in my forehead were severed to the point that when they sewed it up I felt nothing. Maybe if I'd have worn a shoulder harness and a helmet much of the damage could have been prevented but then again maybe nothing could have stopped that piece of metal from being driven through my scalp."

Then Hans reached down to pat the huge yellow Lab puppy that was under his chair and said, "That's why I pick up all the stray dogs that people dump out on the airport road that they don't want anymore, but old Hans wants them. If it hadn't been for those dogs on that line I wouldn't be here today."

There was a complete silence for a minute and then everyone was congratulating Hans that he had survived this terrible ordeal. He shook his head and laughed and said, "It was all a matter of luck. That scar doesn't seem to bother the girls at all."

II

OF CHILDREN AND SOLDIERS

The drive from Victoria to the Refugio Airport seems endless as you cross the flat expanse of flat desert like land. Then you drive through the gate and there are Hans and Ruth's dogs all stacked up in the shade by the hangar. Four big shaggy dogs are standing in the back of an old station wagon patiently waiting for somebody to give them a ride or to go fuel up an airplane.

It's good to get in out of the hot sun and scrounge in the cooler for a cold drink. Then you can squash down in one of the comfy leather chairs and it's quiet and peaceful. Hans comes in from the hangar and has to wipe grease and sweat from his face and hands, then greets all of us with a big grin.

Everyone chatted and then in no time the conversation turned to stories about the past and when Hans was a little kid living in Holland when the Nazis took over during WWII. He said, "I was only four years old when the Germans took over Holland and we little kids had a great time running around in the streets as we were not in school yet. We were not afraid of the German soldiers. They were on patrol in the streets and would ask us to go into the shops to buy them cigarettes and then we could have the change for candy. I was so young that it was above my head to see any danger or trouble but the older folks suffered so much."

"My father was an administrator for a labor organization and it wasn't political even though he was in the labor movement. He looked after the welfare of the men in the transport union and he organized tours, got them into book clubs, weekend trips to historical sites, walking and hiking trips in areas where there was something to be learned. My father was not interested in flying and he never talked to me about flying. He did have a thorough High School education and knew much more than the average man. My father died during the war but my mother and sister still live there. My mother lives close to Amsterdam in Utrecht which is a railroad hub and is in the center of Holland. My sister still lives there. Holland is small and is crisscrossed with lakes and train tracks but I was fortunate that there was an airport about fifteen kilometers (ten miles) from my house so I used to ride my bicycle out there."

"I had skipped one year of high school because I took extra courses and then went to Aeronautical College and skipped a year there. I wanted to get all the education I could and as quickly as possible as my mother didn't have much money so I knew I had to do it on scholarships. I always wanted to be top dog in my classes and my teachers seemed to want to help me get ahead quickly. I finished Aeronautical College when I was eighteen and went into the service which is required in Holland and then all I had left to do was the practical year and I automatically became a technical officer. Then I switched over to pilot training as I already had several hundred hours as a pilot both in sailplanes and power planes. I was very fortunate because flying was very, very expensive in Holland. Since I was one of the very few pilots that had all this experience I was the one chosen to fly for people that wanted to rent a plane for a business trip or to go somewhere on weekends."

During the high school years Hans said that he wasn't much of one for going out to parties and going around for a good time. He said, "I built model airplanes when I was young and joined a model airplane club. I was lucky enough to get acquainted with a KLM (the Dutch Airlines) captain and spent weekends working at the local soaring club hangar. At the age of fourteen I had became a soaring pilot and found it to be a lifelong joy over the years to take flight and leave the Refugio Airport behind and soar high over the Texas countryside."

"I did a lot of traveling in Europe on summer vacations and holidays. I went on my bicycle and traveled to Denmark and spent several weeks there. Denmark is very much like Holland with low country and mostly farming. Another summer I went to the Pyrenees and of course I didn't go across the Pyrenees on my bicycle. We made it to the South of France and spent five weeks getting there and then getting back. One week of that time we helped get in the harvest in southern France to make a little bit of money."

"You understand that during high school in Holland we had to learn several languages. The last years in public school we had already learned French and then in high school we learned English, French and German so that when you finished you had four languages, total. Now, you didn't go into literature in those languages, only grammar. The summer I spent in France helped me become fluent in French and then I worked one summer in Germany at a sailplane repair shop and learned to speak German as well as anybody. The ability to speak other languages gives you a leg up when you are flying to other countries. Of course it does!"

III

CADET MILITARY TRAINING MOOSE JAW, CANADA

"I was flying gliders at the age of fourteen and had my pilot's license by my 18th birthday and at the age of twenty I was inducted into the Royal Dutch Military. I was given a commission as an officer in the Royal Dutch Air Force and during this training I flew jet aircraft. Then I was sent to Canada for further training as an Air Force pilot."

"The military life is strange to me for many reasons. Maybe because first and foremost I'm an individualist and maybe it's me that doesn't fit into their scheme of things. When I arrived in Canada for cadet training most of my instructors were British. They had all this military spick and span stuff. Like spick and span shoes, spick and span lockers and on and on. As I said that is just not Hans' way of living. Maybe the main thing they disliked about me is that I wore the red beret that I had earned in Holland going through the paratrooper training. I had made several hundred jumps and I felt I had earned the right to wear it no matter what. I'm sure it was a status symbol to match the big head it was on! I also wore the Parachuting Wings on my shirt pocket that I had earned and no cadets wore them. Only the pilots wore wings. At seventeen you really ask for a lot of grief, don't you?"

"The Canadians had the authority to discipline me and what they favored for punishment was that I should spend my spare time night or day polishing airplanes. Now the Canadian airplanes were not painted and were highly polished and in the fourteen months I spent there I learned how they kept them that way. Do you know that when my time was up there and I had graduated I still had eighty days of polishing left to do? You can laugh but I was so happy when they waived it."

"The barracks were a problem also. In the room that I was assigned to there were three other guys. One Brit, a Canadian and a Turk. They wanted to split us up probably so the Canadian could report on us. Of course, the British guy was Mr. Spick and Span and the Turk was an old guy. He must have been thirty and was already an Army officer. He was a Major in his own country and left us pretty well alone and that was a relief as it seemed everybody took all of their spite out on the cadets."

"But during the training a fantastic thing happened. When I was transferred from Centralia to the Cadet training they also transferred the same flight instructor that I had had there. He was from South Africa and an ex-RAF pilot and I got along fine with him. There was another guy, a particular sergeant that ended up having to be my supervisor as I was doing all this polishing and this poor guy was pulled away from his home life to be sure that I was polishing. He would always ask me, "When are your days up?" and I would say, "Well, I think I just have another twenty-three days to go. I really felt sorry for this guy as he was the only non-commissioned officer there and he was stuck with the cadets. In fact, he was so stuck with me that between Christmas and New Years he even took me home with him and we would go out to the hanger after dinner and he would help me polish. We would both work like crazy as fast as we could and then we'd retire back at his house and watch television until it was time for me to go back to the barracks. He would even drive me back so that I wouldn't be late and get more polishing time. It was more of a punishment for him than me because he wanted to be at home with his wife. See what I mean about military life?"

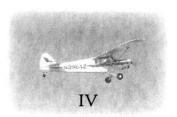

IV

HAULING ALONG AFTER A U.S. NAVY COMMANDER

"During our T-6 training we had what you call a mid-term leave. Half of our training was finished and after the leave you would continue with instrument training, gunnery, precision flying and all that. The leave was for ten days. Fortunately for me they waived my polishing time and let me go. Well, all the cadets had gotten together and had put up a pot where everybody had to put in a couple of dollars and the cadet who went the furthest from Moose Jaw, Saskatchewan (which is out in the middle of nowhere) would win the pot. Some of the students were saying they were going to the East coast and of course daddy was paying. People were going wherever by train, by bus, by boat or wherever they had the money to go. Money was always a problem for me and I had to decide quickly how far I could get by hitch-hiking. Unlike the other cadets who were only Sgt's. I was a Second Lt. because I had finished my training as a technical officer. I ended up by hitch-hiking to North Dakota to a Military Strategic Air Command Air Base and got a ride to Japan. Yahoo, I was on my way! Oh, to prove that you really went to the destination you were claiming you would have to mail a letter back to our base. I arrived in Japan on the third day of my leave and had seven days left to get back to base. It was beautiful and no problem. However, the Korean War was over and there were very few planes coming back from Japan. You had to have some sort of priority to get a ride back and so I was getting worried. I wasn't as worried about myself as I was about the other fellows in my unit. What really worried me was what the Canadian authorities would think in regard to Holland after spending all the money training me. So I decided that before the time was up to be back I would send a telegram to my commanding officer. I told him that I was stuck in Japan and that I would make it back as soon as I could get a ride and that I was sorry."

"Immediately the wheels started to turn. Even at that big base when they found out that I was a cadet and that I had to be back on time or else! But they were not happy with me since there was no way of getting any priority pass and because I didn't even belong to the American forces."

"I ended up getting a ride with a U.S. Navy Commander who was making an inspection tour of the Far East. That Navy Commander made me his aide because I was already an officer. We would stop at all these various islands and I would haul along behind him and we would inspect the troops. Then we would inspect all of the facilities on that island. Of course, I was treated very well hauling along after the Commander. It took us three weeks to complete the inspection tour and to get back to the United States."

"In San Diego they arranged for my transportation back to Moose Jaw. They arranged a special cross-country flight for one of their staff pilots who needed flight time and we flew in a T-33 back to Canada. The Navy pilot asked the tower, as we were coming in, for transportation for two officers to get to base headquarters. The tower answered that there would be transportation for one officer and one prisoner to be taken to confinement. When we landed they promptly locked me up. After things settled down it was decided that they would let me stay in the cadets and that I could graduate. I had a little bit of a hard time for a couple weeks with the ground school, but I easily caught up on the courses and here again my aeronautical training came to my aid. I had more flight training time than any of the other cadets and I was lucky to get the same instructor back and he was lenient about my escapade. Everything worked out and I won the pot also."

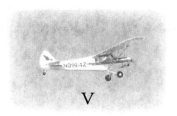

V

SURVIVAL TRAINING IN THE STICKS OF CANADA

"I had another memorable event during the survival training. We were in the ready room and you are dressed in your uniform with your flight coveralls over that. This room is where the pilots sit and wait for their flights. It was summertime and I hadn't put on my uniform under the coveralls and had only my underwear on. You might know that I was picked and I didn't have any of the regulation equipment with me either. I ran from the ready room and they hauled me off in a bus with nine other people from various flights. Then they flew us to northern Canada and we landed somewhere in the sticks and there a helicopter flew us to another remote area. There we were split up and in our group of four there was a Turk, a British and another Canadian. I was in pretty sad shape with no survival gear. Not even a pocket knife or matches. All I had was my underwear and my flight-suit. It was midsummer and so during the day it was alright but the whole idea is to survive in the bush and more importantly make your way out."

"After four hours of hard walking we came across a creek. In northern Canada all of the rivers run into the Arctic and I assumed that the smaller creeks would run into the bigger ones and then on into a river and at the river there would be a settlement. I decided that this would be the easiest way to get out even though it meant going further north. This creek was deep enough to float a raft so the Turk and I decided to build one. The Turk had most of his equipment so we would have what we needed to fashion our craft. We gathered light limbs and using parts of the Turks flight suit we tied it all together and finally had a usable raft."

"One of the pilots had a crude map and the two of them decided to try it on foot going south. We waited until the next morning and then started floating downstream and by late afternoon we had already come up to a settlement. It was small with just a couple of Indian families. To me our problems were over and I didn't intend to go any farther. I figured that if the Indians could live there, we could too. We couldn't talk to the Indians as they were Chippewa but they took care of us. I went fishing with them and started to find out how they did their daily work. We ate fish and rabbit and some moose. We were being monitored from above by the Canadian Air Force. They probably were trying to figure out how long we were going to stay put. We had already been there three days and I wasn't going to go anywhere and the Turk had decided to stick it out with me. Finally, they came and picked us up in a helicopter and I don't think they were thrilled by our easy survival. All this training did become important when I later flew as a bush pilot over vast stretches of uninhabited land."

VI

THE WILDS OF CANADA AND
A TICKET TO NOWHERE

"I was out of the Dutch Air Force and twenty years old and my whole life was out there somewhere just waiting to be lived. I knew that it would be flying and it couldn't be in Holland because Holland is too small of a country, being only 160 miles long and 100 miles wide there are no flying jobs. I know an American can't really understand how really small that is in comparison to the United States"

"I went to the immigration service and applied to three countries, Canada, Brazil and Australia. I had decided that whichever paperwork came through first that's where I would go. Fortunately, for me it was Canada and I immediately sold everything I owned, a motorcycle and books and wound up with enough money to book passage on a boat. The crossing took ten days and we docked at Quebec City. The Canadian Government gave me a railroad ticket to any destination that I chose and $50.00 to get going. I bought a ticket to Vancouver because Vancouver was on the opposite side of the country and that way

I could travel across the entire country and get off wherever I wanted to."

"Two weeks after leaving Quebec City reality set in. I stopped at several places trying to find a job and couldn't find anything because all I had was my Canadian pilot's license. I had never done any manual labor in my life and there were no flying jobs to be had. The train stopped in Edmonton, Alberta and I was really desperate as my money was gone. I went to immigration service and told them about the predicament I was in and they told me to go to the Youth Hall, similar to the YMCA. The next afternoon I went back to the employment office and they said there was only one job opening and that was with a lumber camp in Northern Alberta. The clerk looked me over and said that I wouldn't make it up there. He said that I wasn't strong or rough enough to do the hard work. I pleaded with him to give me the job and that I could do it. After about an hour of my badgering him and arguing with him they gave me the railroad ticket and I boarded a train that evening for my new life as a lumberjack."

"This was a very, very slow train and it stopped at every little settlement and delivered mail and freight. It was spring and all I had with me was a duffle bag and it was pretty cold as we were going north and I was shivering in the passenger car. Finally the conductor came through the car and yelled, "Passenger for Demmit, Alberta get off at the next stop". When we arrived he said, "Off you go" and off I got. There was no station, no platform to wait on and so I just stood next to the tracks and watched the train disappear into the distance. The sun was slowly setting and I wondered what I would do if night fell and nobody came to pick me up. I decided that this was the way they got rid of foreigners by just shipping them off to the boonies. I was sure that was the end of the line for me."

"Dusk was settling all around me as I sat on my duffle bag waiting for what seemed to be hours. Then I heard the rumbling of a truck coming up the track and somebody was laying on the horn. When it stopped beside me this old guy leaned out and asked if I was going to work at the lumber camp and I said, "Yes" and he said, "Get in."

"The lumber camp had a small sawmill and now it was spring and they were sawing and planing the lumber that they had cut during the winter. My first job was to load the farm wagons with the rough lumber and then in a few weeks they had me loading boxcars. Then I was promoted to be the planer man. The reality of what hard manual work really meant came to me at that time. My hands were all scraped and broken with blisters that would seep blood all over everything. Lots of lumber went out of there with old Hans' blood marking it. There was salvation as several weeks later my hands toughened up and I felt I was as good as anybody else there. The pay at that time was 85 cents an hour for everybody in the camp, except the planer man got a little more pay and I was the planer man. We worked ten hours a day for a total of $8.50 a day and they deducted $2.50 a day for room and board so we made a grand total of $6.00 a day."

"The big event every two weeks was that after we got paid we'd all take the long trip to town. I was so happy on the first trip to buy flannel long johns and some shirts and jeans. I needed loggers work boots and heavy gloves."

"A German immigrant was running the lumber camp and he found out after a few weeks that I was educated and could do more than just load boxcars and he put me to work for three hours every night in the office doing the payroll. This was really a break for me because I had to know what I was reading in English and be accurate with the payroll books. Up to this time I had not had the need to speak English well and read with understanding."

VII

JOE GAMBLER, JIM GAMBLER AND LOUIE GAMBLER

"Several Cree Indians worked with us and to get away from the camp once in awhile I would go with them to their reservation. They were superb horsemen and taught me to ride horse-back and I found that I was really pretty good at staying aboard while riding through the dense woods and up the steep mountain sides. Some of these boys were rodeo performers and rode all over western Canada during the rodeo season."

"They had been given names at the camp and all had Gambler for a last name. There was Joe Gambler, Jim Gambler, Louie Gambler and all answered to Gambler."

"The name calling was so hilarious at times and dispelled the monotony of our long work days and they would join in the laughter and call us weird Indian names. I'm sure these names could possibly have meant animal excrement if we had known. And they did love to gamble and at the drop of a hat they would throw down money to bet on some crazy thing."

"The only big town that was close to our camp was Dawson

Creek on the Alaskan Highway and while there one weekend I found a small airport with a flight school. I was amazed at my good luck and immediately started work on my private pilot's license. During that summer of 1957 I took the written exam and the flight test and then my main objective was to get my Canadian Commercial pilot's license and seaplane rating to qualify me to fly in northern Canada. Now my work at the lumber camp became easier as I had a real need for the money to further my pilot training and ratings."

"I worked at the lumber camp until winter and when things froze over and they were getting ready to go into the woods to go lumbering I decided to quit. I was in better shape than I had ever been because of the physical labor and the food which was excellent and healthy but I knew that I wasn't fit enough to run those big saws around the clock in the freezing cold weather. I had found out about a school where I could obtain my Canadian Commercial license out in Western Ontario. I made a deal with the instructor there that if I came down there and paid for my training he would give me a job working at the airport to pay for my room and board."

"It was the middle of December when I arrived there and the deal had fallen through already. I continued on towards Toronto to see if I could find a job there. I found a job with Massey-Ferguson as an assembler making farm combines and that ended in six months and so I went on to Kingston, Ontario. I worked there for six months as a quality inspector in a battery factory. Finally, I had saved up enough money to finish my commercial training and went to Chatham, Ontario where I flew Aeronca Champions, Cessna 120's and a Cessna 195. Then I went on to northern Ontario, an area of lakes, and went with a commercial outfit that had a flight school and there I received my seaplane rating."

VIII

AEROBATICS AND THE OLD INVERTED HANKY TRICK

"The only job that I could find there was managing a small airport at St. Thomas, Ontario. They had been running a flying service there and the company had dissolved and slowly all the people went on to work at other places. That left me running the place for the town which still had a contract to fulfill. During all this time my main objective was to fly as many hours as I could and I rented airplanes from some of the private plane owners. I built up my time and talked to these pilots trying to find out all I could about flying in Canada. I bought an old Canadian trainer, a Fairchild PT-26 from the Canadian Mounted Police. When I had money for gasoline I flew that airplane every morning the remainder of that spring and fall and practiced aerobatics"

"I had gone to several aerobatic air shows and had seen the Inverted Hanky Trick. I decided to get a whole routine worked up of daredevil flying. I probably had the idea that I could do almost anything."

"On the outskirts of the airport was a farmers' field and there was an old Studebaker sitting there. I thought of a routine I had seen where a European aerobatic pilot removed a handkerchief off the roof of a car with his wingtip. I knew I could master this trick with a little practice so I attached a welding rod on the wingtip of my airplane so that I had about a two and a half foot margin of error when trying to pick up the hanky. When I touched the handkerchief with the rod it would just flutter to the ground and in exasperation I cut the welding rod shorter and shorter until I had just a few inches left on it."

"Early one morning after daybreak I was practicing. There was no turbulence and I thought I was getting much better in judging my distance from the wingtip to the car. But judgment went right out the window as the wingtip hit the roof of the car and not only that but it broke the rear window right out of the car. I remember seeing the ground coming up as the airplane cart-wheeled over and then for some strange reason I continued flying except ninety degrees in the other direction. I managed to get the airplane on the ground and found there was quite a bit of damage to the wingtip."

"I didn't know that every day when I was practicing this hanky car trick that I had an audience watching me from the coffee shop across the airport. The cook and early waitress were betting on how long it would be until I would do myself in. They got all that for free! Shortly after that I sold the plane as it just didn't appeal to me anymore"

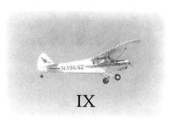

IX

MISSIONARY WORK IN CANADA
– LIVING WITH THE INDIANS

"A beautiful Cessna 170 with a Franklin engine flew in one day and the gentleman who stepped out of it told me that the plane had this unusual engine because it was outfitted for missionary work in northern Canada. When he found out that I was neither a smoker nor a drinker he offered me a job of flying for them in Northern Alberta in the Indian Country. These were Mennonites from Pennsylvania and Iowa and they had several mission posts where they ran schools, public health stations and stores."

"That was the winter of 1958 and I went to work for them and enjoyed the flying but the pay was nonexistent. These people had a Piper PA-12 Super-Cruiser and the Cessna 170. I was getting plenty of flying time as we were flying both airplanes. We flew the missionaries in and out and tons of supplies. In the summer the place was completely inaccessible and all the dry goods and supplies were flown in during the winter and stockpiled. We used skis on the planes because all the settlements in the north-country are on a lake or a river. You have to be careful because you don't have any brakes and you have to time it right in order to stop."

"There is the hardship during the winter of starting the airplane and getting it going in the morning because it is so very cold. You have to have an engine tent and put a heater in it and then you have to stay with it all night because of the fire hazard and oil and gas leaking. Even so in the morning you have to warm up the engine and warm up the oil before you get going. The job gave me plenty of experience and flying time that I needed and gave me exposure to the commercial operators that were flying in the area."

"I suddenly realized that if I ever had to go down in the North I could live off the land because of all the different types of work that I had done and all the things people had taught me that I had met. Working with Indians and living with them in the woods, trapping animals for food and learning the ways that they hunted and lived off the land had taught me skills that I knew that I could survive. Whenever I couldn't fly I went into the woods with the Indians and learned how to trap the bigger animals as well as the smaller."

"In order to catch animals in the snow you use snare wires. The animals make paths in the snow and keep using these paths so you simply set the snares out wherever you see their prints. Then you can go about the business of gathering wood and you build a shelter and usually when you go back you will have something in the snare. You have to know how to skin expertly and then cook the meat carefully to avoid getting sick. We were trapping for furs and I was using the money to live on just like the Indians as the missionaries just didn't have the money to give me a decent wage."

X

HAULING FISH FOR A REAL PAYCHECK

"The next year, 1959, a commercial operator looked me up and offered me a job flying for pay! I started flying Cessna 180's, a Stinson and all other types of general aviation airplanes. We flew the Cessna 195's with wheels, skis and floats. We did all kinds of jobs from hauling fresh fish out of lakes to the market for the fishermen and then hauling frozen fish for the fish processing plants. We hauled all kinds of people from government officials to a traveling judge who went to all of the settlements. We flew geologists, oil company people, surveyors and anyone having to do business in the North Country. The airplane is the only mode of travel in the North Country even in the summertime."

"In the summer the land thaws out but the frost will stay in the ground and as only the first six feet thaws out it gets very swampy. You can't drive a vehicle on that and so it's only in the winter time when this frost layer called Muskeg is frozen again that the oil companies can get in there and take in their heavy drilling equipment. They have to get out before summer arrives and get all the heavy equipment out because if they left it there it would break through the frost layer and sink."

"I worked for several other commercial flying operators after that and wound up working for a company called 'Alberta Fish Products' which owned a fish processing plant. I flew an airplane that was the same age as I was. The airplane was an old Fairchild 82 and was built in 1936 and it was a big airplane – 600 HP and could carry a 3000 + load and it was not at all unusual on skis to be hauling 4000 pounds of freight. We were mainly hauling fish out from this big plant but with people working in it we hauled tons of groceries in and tons of fish out. We hauled diesel fuel, oil and gasoline for the outboard motors and power plant fuel. Canada had a system where a certain lake would be fished out to the limit and then they would clean it out and restock with better fish. The Fisheries Department of Northern Canada used this method to upgrade many large lakes.

XI

LAC LA BICHE – ALBERTA, CANADA

"I was living during the winter with a commercial fisherman as there were very few places to stay at Beaver Lake in northern Alberta and I had a room and had my meals there. His wife was British and she taught school in Lac La Biche seven miles away and so she was up early and gone and we rarely saw her during the week."

"We were flying the crated fish from different distant lakes and often came home late at night and too late for dinner. We would just make ourselves at home and raid the refrigerator for the leftovers and drag out this conglomeration of cheese and cold meat or whatever looked edible. One evening we found this dish with slices of meat and it looked like liverwurst to me and I'm just crazy about that so we made ourselves some big thick sandwiches with it and added some pickles. The next day we packed a lunch to take with us and added some more of those good sandwiches. That evening we got home long past dinner time and I could hear Becky moving around in the next room so I called to her and asked, "Becky do you have some more of that sandwich loaf left that we had last night?" She called back, "Yes, there is some of that same stuff you guys ate yesterday." So we made ourselves some more sandwiches and got some beer and sat down on the couch and then she pokes her head out of her door and says, "Woof, woof!" The next morning very early we could hear her barking like a crazy woman as she walked to her car. Then her husband started telling us how the dog food kept disappearing out of the refrigerator."

"We liked Becky well enough but she was always complaining about us and our messy habits so now with the dog food business we planned to get even with her. She was always accusing us of running around with wild women so we decided on a scheme to really upset her. She did our laundry so we would put little note papers in our shirt pockets with this phone number on it and on the inside of a matchbook cover I scribbled the same number with a heart on it. She finds all these little pieces of paper with this same phone number in our shirts in the laundry so puts it together and can't stand the suspense so she calls the number. She listens carefully to see who will answer and then it comes, City of Tarnette Dog Pound".

"She had a very hot temper and if she hadn't blown up and told it around town, we wouldn't have known how really mad she was. She did clean out the refrigerator and it was bare for a whole week."

XII

SWEETGRASS LANDING – CANADA

"The next job I had was at Sweetgrass Landing flying Helio Couriers and we were in the Wood Buffalo Park which is a very large wildlife preserve. My job was herding buffalo with the airplane. Buffalo are just like cattle and they are not the sharpest animals in the world. In the early fall when the rivers and lakes were starting to freeze over the buffalo would try to cross the ice and of course would fall through. One would fall in and start to holler and then the rest of them would come running to the rescue. The previous year they had hundreds of animals drown this way or freezing to death. So my job, depending upon how quick the water would freeze solid enough to hold the buffalo was to keep them as far away as possible. It was a real crazy job keeping animals moving with an airplane. I flew right along beside them to keep them moving and then I would fly back and forth to pick up the stragglers and get them back in the herd."

"I observed a strange governmental project go into effect at this same time. They were trying to get the natural balance of predators away from the buffalo and their main natural enemy is the wolf. The job of the game warden was to get rid of the wolves so they were shot at out of airplanes and killed. They were tracked on the ground with snow mobiles and they did a very thorough job. The next year there were so few wolves to weed out the sick and weak buffalo from the herd and as a result Anthrax broke out. The Anthrax killed all of the buffalo except for two small groups that were not with the big herd. This happened in 1961 and for years and years now they have been working desperately to bring the herd back to where it was. They lost 90% of the herd that time and just because of stupidity."

"Years later in 1967 I was back in Canada flying for a summer and ended up flying an airplane down to Ft. Williams to have floats installed and then we were going to fly on to Guyana. I was flying over an island in one of the great lakes close to the Canadian border called Ile Royale. It is so isolated there and the Canadians have been doing a study that combined the moose and wolf populations. They have left them alone and amazingly the populations have stabilized themselves into approximately the same number of animals in each group. The study has been going on for a long time and does show that man should leave well enough alone and let nature find its balance."

"We had a terrible fire in the camp and all the paper work on the airplanes and all my log books were lost. I was married when this happened and all of our clothes and belongs were gone and we still had several months left of winter. We would have to buy all new winter clothing and that would be so expensive and I was tired of living that way. I wanted a trip to Europe and wanted to see my mother in Holland. I had been in Canada six years and had become a Canadian citizen during that time but felt it was time to go home and take a much needed vacation. Out of that trip to Europe came the trip to Africa."

XIII

GOING BACK HOME IS DIFFERENT AND A VACATION IN SPAIN

"Going back home is always different than you have anticipated. After six years of being away I was remembering only the good things and had forgotten the bad. I had forgotten how really bad the weather is at this time of the year in Holland and we minded the cold and damp and the rain. We were used to the cold but liked the sunny and dry weather in Canada. My wife couldn't understand my mother's Dutch at all and with the weather problems we stayed only a week in Utrecht. I had planned to go back to Canada when the float plane season began about the tenth of May and I had a job lined up for that time. It was going to be a long time for us to wait until May and we craved a sunny place to vacation and decided to go to Spain. Spain was still the cheapest place in Europe to vacation and the weather is beautiful in Southern Spain along the Mediterranean."

"We bought a little Volkswagon and drove to a little fishing village along the Spanish coast. We found a stone villa high on a slope overlooking the blue Mediterranean. The Spanish labor was cheap when they built these beauties with Terrazzo floors throughout and arched windows and doors that let in the sea breeze. There was no roadway going to the villa and you had to park your car at the top of the cliff and then go down the narrow path to your house."

"There we spent our time basking in the sun on the beaches and every night I'd go out with the Sardine fishermen in their little boats and we'd sit and fish and drink wine and break bread."

"Six weeks had passed and it was March and I was tired of fishing with the Sardine fishermen. I was tired of lying around on the beach every day. I wanted to fly. I needed to fly so I went to the local airport."

"I took the copies of my Canadian licenses but I had no log books or anything to support the hours that I had flown. Everything had been lost in the Canadian fire but I did have a statement from the Canadian authorities recording how much time that they knew of that I had flown in Canada. I had renewed my instructors rating and had the date when I had taken my commercial license exam and had records of all the different ratings."

"The flying in Spain at that time was all military and all the flying clubs at the airport were military but I did manage to rent this acrobatic airplane anyway, a Bucker Jungmeister."

"It felt so good to be in a plane again and as I took off and climbed toward the sun I thought it would be a clever idea to go over and give the fishermen over at our village a little bit of a show. So I buzzed our villa and got right down on the beach and buzzed those fishermen right out of their little boats. I did some aerobatics over them and the town and then flew back to the airport and got my car and drove home. When I got to the house I saw our only neighbor coming up our path toward me."

"He was very British and was wearing his knickerbockers. This man was an elegant gray haired fellow in his early sixties and as he approached he said, "Oh, and you are the young chap flying over the beach this morning?" My only response to that was, "Yes sir!" He introduced himself and told me that he was

Air Commodore Mitchell. He wanted to know what kind of work that I had been doing and I told him about my military experience in Holland and my training in Canada and about my flying in the bush for five years and he listened intently. He was silent for a moment and then came up with this statement and said that he knew of a place where my talents could be used. He expanded on this by telling me that he had recently flown Prince Phillip into Kenya in 1963 on a hunting trip and they had flown all over East Africa together. He had flown for the Wilken Air Service and that the chief pilot there was John Falconer Taylor. You would be in awe of this if you were British. He paused then as if to give me time to take all this in and then continuing he said that he was the Commander of the Queen's Flight! I was so awe struck then because flying for the Queen of England would be compared to flying Air Force One for the President of the United States."

"He went on to say that he was on vacation time and had been bored to tears until he saw the air show this morning. We talked for a couple of hours and he told me that he was certain that there was a good job for me flying in Africa. I told him that I didn't know anything about Africa and that I had a job waiting for me in Canada. As he was leaving he said, "You'll hear from me."

"And sure enough a few days later he came by with a telegram from Africa saying that I had been hired. The telegram said that the job was a two-year contract and I saw that the salary was double what I had been making when I left Canada. The company was in Kenya and had made arrangements for me to go to London and had booked passage to East Africa".

"We packed our bags and drove back to Holland and all the way we talked about Africa and looked at maps and I tried to imagine how it would be flying in such a different environment."

HANS WITH SMITH MINI-PLANE

AERONCA CHAMP, HANS IN CANADA

CESSNA 180 SPRAYER WHILE SPRAYING IN AFRICAN HIGHLANDS

GRUMMAN WIDGEON HANS IS PREPARING
TO FERRY TO FLORIDA TO AFRICA

DeHavilland Beaver on floats in Canada

Britton Norman transport in Canada

HANS REFUELING M-AIR SPRAY PLANE PRIOR TO FLIGHT

HANS IN SPRAY PLANE, THE LAST PLANE HE FERRIED
ACROSS THE ATLANTIC TO SALISBURY, AFRICA

Sailplane – Hans ready to soar at Refugio County Airport

Early VANAIR Services sign, Refugio County Airport

HANS WITH PIPER PAWNEE CROP DUSTER
AT REFUGIO COUNTY AIRPORT.

XIV

FLYING IN AFRICA 1964

"We flew into Nairobi and I was so surprised at the modern airport with just beautiful buildings and everything just spick and span. We found that the weather was superb with warm days and cool nights because of the elevation which was 4500 ft. above sea level."

"The company gave me time to convert my licenses to East African and then all I needed was the letter from the Canadian authorities stating that I had the minimum flying time. I was really starting my flying career all over again as far as the log book and it seemed strange to me that it should be in Africa."

"The first day on the job I found that it was a large company and that there were fifteen other pilots working there. They were flying a conglomeration of airplanes. They had five single engine Comanche's, several Cherokees and Aztecs and for training purposes they had Tripacers and Colts. They used a few Super Cubs for anti-poaching and game surveys. Not one person talked to me or advised me on what I was supposed to be doing on that first day. So I went on my own to the local aviation authority that handled the licensing and did the written exams. I showed them the list I had made showing all the flying experience I had and showed them the letters from the Canadian government confirming the time that I had flown in Canada."

"I had felt very helpless without my log books and credentials. Finally, I had my Commercial pilot's license for the different types of planes that I wanted to fly and did get my instructors rating on the basis of what the papers said from Canada. I tried to stay busy while I was waiting for the company to put me to work and tell me where I was going. I did checkouts in Super Cubs and I flew with some of the pilots so that I could get to know the local area."

"The country around Nairobi is the most beautiful place you would ever hope to see. All the way to the Indian Ocean and on to Mombassa and on towards Tanzania and the highlands are the most beautiful sights in the world. Mount Kilimanjaro is incredible to see from the air and the coffee plantations at Moshi are expanses of green as far as the eye can see."

"All of this time nobody had talked to me other than the chief pilot and he ordered me not to mention how much my salary was to the other pilots, as I was making more than they were. Calling them local pilots was wrong because they were expatriates. Mostly British, with three Australians, a few South Africans and two Rhodesians. They were all white and we had no black pilots until the following year when the company did have to hire them."

"I went to the chief pilot to find out when I was going to start flying as I was going crazy here with nothing to do. He told me that I would be flying Cessna 180's and did I think I could fly those. I said, "Yes sir, and I can fly anything that you have here." I waited another ten days and then a man flew down to see me. His name was 'Eton", Major John Eton. Major Eton ran the base of operations in Somalia which is the country just north of Kenya."

"The reason our company had a base there is that after Somalia became independent the British left Northern Somalia and the Italians left Southern Somalia and that left nobody to run the flying service. We were there to support the exploration efforts of the Sinclair Oil Company and the Gulf Oil Company. Because of our companies presence there as a commercial flying operation we started picking up some more aid and they were building a harbor in Kismayu to the south of Mogadisu. They were building a tuna processing plant in the Horn of Africa which was five-hundred miles to the north at the northeast point of the African peninsula."

"Finally, I was told that I would be taking over the base of operations at Mogadisu and my instructions were to pack my belongings and take my wife and hurry up and get there. I was happy with the thought that I would be going to work and anxious to get to the flying."

"It was the middle of June when we headed out for Mogadisu. I couldn't fly it non-stop as the trip was over six hundred miles and I planned to make the one fuel stop. There would be no border problems and I would have to go through customs at Wilson Airport in Nairobi and then customs in Mogadisu. I landed at a place called Garissa for refueling and had been warned not to land too far down the strip because the Kenya army was at their post only at the end of the strip and they couldn't guarantee my safety at the far end. They had been having a problem with border bandits called Shifta. This was my first indication that flying in this territory was not going to be all that uneventful."

"We did arrive safely in Mogadisu and the local leader there showed me our transportation, a scooter and told me where to find the house that we were going to occupy. I was ready to settle in and get to work."

"I found I was flying the Cessna 180's quite a bit. We were averaging six to seven hours a day and that was every day. Also, I found that there weren't any weekends. The Arabs had no weekends as their day off is Friday and that made Saturday and Sunday into workdays. We flew on the weekends for the local Somali people. After about six months another pilot came to help me as we were flying more than we could handle. We had one spare airplane in Nairobi being serviced so that we were ever ready for hundred hour inspection. One pilot would fly to Nairobi and load the airplane with fresh meat and vegetables and all the produce that are not obtainable in the desert country like Somalia. Then that pilot would turn right around and come back with the plane that just had the 100 hour inspection. We had hardly any down time. That trip to Nairobi is a 1200 mile trip with a one hour stop to load up and get airborne again."

"The airport in Somalia was controlled by the military and therefore all communications of any kind, the radio, telephone, telegraph and all flying was handled through them. Subsequently, the U.S. Aid gave the Somali government two airplanes, DC-3's Douglas Dakotas and they started to run a local airline with those. Until then the only outside air service we had was that once a week Alitalia would fly in with a DC-7 all the way from Rome. The plane came in on a Saturday evening and left again on Sunday morning. Two times a week Adin Airways DC-3 would make a stop on the way from Adin to Nairobi. Air traffic control was virtually non-existent except for our airport tower at Mogadisu. It was operated by a hand crank transmitter, with a guy sitting on a sand dune with a parasol over his head and when he heard an airplane coming he'd crank up this radio."

"The only safety feature that we had when flying over the desert was high frequency radios. With these long distance radios we could contact Addis Ababa, the Ethiopian control center which was run by Americans TWA Ethiopia and then the British in Edin and the British in Nairobi. So through the HF radio system we could file flight plans and make people aware of where we were going in the event that anything would happen to us enroute. With the flight plan already sent out on the HF radio system the British would handle the search and rescue and would cover the whole territory."

XV

THE MIRAGE

"The second year that I was in the desert country I had two pilots working with me. One was an American pilot that had requested a job with us and he had experience flying the Cessna 180 and had flown in Somalia. This fellow was very short and it made it very hard for him in adverse conditions to operate a tail wheel airplane such as a Cessna 180. The trips inland had little more of a danger factor and I would normally take all of these trips. The easier trips were flying along the coast where the populated centers were and I had the other pilots fly these."

"On one particular day I had an extended trip of two days with a ministerial party that included some government politicians. They were making a tour of the interior which is desert country. It was about 5:30 in the afternoon and I was getting ready to land in Hargeisha in northern Somalia when I got word from Adin control that one of our airplanes was down. I had this feeling that it might be our American pilot because he had been on his way to Arigavo which is also in Northern Somalia. If he had taken a direct line from Mogadisu he would have had to fly over Ethiopian territory and apparently on his way back from Arigavo with his passengers worried about being over hostile territory. He might have gotten confused to the point that he made the decision to make a landing so he could find out exactly where he was. Radio control said that after they had received the message that the aircraft was presumed to be down that they didn't have any more radio contact with them."

"I landed in Hargeisha and refueled and then talked to radio control by reeling out the antenna and setting up communications. They had an idea of where they thought the aircraft could have gone down and they had his flight plan with the time of departure given. It seemed such poor planning to me as it would be almost impossible to make the complete flight during the daylight hours. I went to the guest house in town and went to bed to get some much needed rest as I planned to search for the missing plane early the next day. I couldn't get to sleep and was lying there thinking about the lost plane and with my eyes closed I tried to envision how the pilot would have been flying from Arigavo on his route. There was a coastal mountain range to cross and from there it was flat desert terrain for about 200 miles. Beyond that there was an area of sandy hills with no vegetation and these hills are very close to the Ethiopian border. In my mind I decided that this would be where he became confused and worried. He was afraid that he had flown into Ethiopian territory. I made the decision that I would fly out to that area in the morning and I left a note for my party of my intentions to leave and to search for the missing plane."

"The next morning I loaded the plane with extra fuel that would enable me to land and refuel if I needed to. Sometimes you had to land out there in any possible landing place and you learned by experience the differences in the landscape and we usually would look for river beds. I figured that if I flew out shortly before daylight I would have plenty of time to fly the 300 miles to where I thought the plane might be down."

"As the morning passed the sun started heating up the ground and then the heat waves would appear which was common every day stuff but it would bother you when you were looking at the horizon because everything in your vision is wavy. It really bothered you when you had to spot something on the sand or a landing place."

"I was looking into the heat waves when I saw a mirage forming. The mirage that appeared showed the downed plane very distinctly and it was lying with one wing tipped up and I saw people walking around it. The landing gear was laying quite a ways from the airplane. The most prominent object in the mirage was a rock and it would keep popping up. This rock was just lying there. The background was made up of a very odd shaped hill. I knew where this hill was because I had seen it before. I changed my course towards that hill and flew directly to the downed airplane."

"The pilot had landed on a dry river bed called a Wadi. The landing was fine and he found out that he was in Somali territory. Then when he took off again he hit the boulder which sheared off the landing gear and the plane tipped with the one wing up. The pilot hit the instrument panel and had a cut on his forehead and also hurt his shoulder. Thankfully, none of the passengers were hurt."

"Mirages have been recorded throughout history and records have shown that you can see an entire town in these visions. In the desert or very hot areas pilots have seen complete cities with towers and buildings and of course they are not there. Most everyone has seen something in the heat waves on a highway as you are traveling in the summer and you might even slow down a little but the vision just keeps appearing on down the road."

"I have no explanation for the clarity of the mirage that I saw because the event had happened the day before and I had not known or heard anything about the accident other than the radio report that the plane was missing. When I think of this accident in the desert I'm always so thankful that I was there to help out."

XVI

GETTING STONED IN SOMALIA

"Most of the flying in Somalia was for the oil and drilling companies and different government agencies. The second year that I was in Somalia our main flying was involved with the Peace Corps and flying the teachers to the interior. The whole program was for instructing the Somalis. The American teachers came in groups of two and were placed in the different schools and we found them places to stay and looked after their transportation and communications. Other than that they were supposed to live the same kind of life as the Somalis."

"The Somalis are Moslems and they thought all the teachers were Christians because they were white. According to the Moslem religion anything they can do to further their beliefs makes them a better Moslem. They carried this to a degree where they might try to do something wrong to a Christian and that automatically makes the act good and they are then a better Moslem. It doesn't make sense to someone from the Western world and that was a problem with the young Peace Corps teachers."

"I had flown into a village in the interior and before dark I decided to take a little stroll down the street where I was staying at a small hotel and even for me who had lived here and knew the Moslem's ways it turned out to be a very wrong thing to do."

"At sundown the Moslems do their worshiping of Allah and seeing this Christian walking down their street and interfering with their worship they proceeded to stone me. The children started it and then the oldsters joined in and pelted me with bigger stones. I was down and would have been stoned to death but a Somalis policeman stepped in and managed to get it stopped. I found out that he had been trained in the U.S. in a police academy and knew better than let them kill me."

"The Peace Corps teachers were running into the same problems. The whole idea was to teach the children and they couldn't get the parents to let them come to school as they thought it was a Christian school."

"Two male Peace Corps workers would naturally room together in a house but this was interpreted by the townsmen as something not normal and they thought it kinky. In a society that is geared to male supremacy everything is male in the Moslem religion and everything is owned by the man in the house and being two guys had no women in the house they didn't like the looks of it. So they had another reason not to send their children to the school. I talked to a police lieutenant in the town and we decided that the reason for the empty classroom was the fact that the two men were living together in the same house. The policeman suggested we move a female teacher in with the men and when we accomplished the move it did take care of the problem very nicely. But then we got a problem of a different nature when two weeks later I got a call on the radio that both teachers had symptoms of VD. They had to go to Mogadisu for treatment."

"These young American idealists came here to change this part of the world and didn't have maturity to cope with the problems of a hostile environment. They strolled around with their beards and cutoffs and one young man even kept a camel for a pet and how do you think that appeared to the Moslems. These youngsters were easily dissolutioned because they came here with such high hopes and were not accepted and found that the Moslems didn't want any part of them. It took a few years for those in Washington to realize that this program was a bust and a waste of money."

"Our charter business fizzled out in Somalia as Sinclair and Gulf Oil finished their exploration as they hadn't been successful with drilling. The U.S. government had sent aide and money to the Somalis and they were setting up their own airline and they thought we were a threat to them. As the Peace Corps dwindled to nothing our company decided to end our operations in Mogadisu."

XVII

SAFARI TOURS AFRICA 1964

"I was transferred to Nairobi and went to work setting up photographic safaris and it involved flying the customers to the game parks. The twenty-one day excursion tour included airfare from America to Africa via London and then we flew them to various game parks for the rest of the time. We spent one day in Nairobi then several days in the Indian Ocean area and then on to Malindi and Membassa then to the game parks in Kenya, Uganda and Tanzania. We as their pilots stayed with the tour all of the time in case of emergency. I couldn't believe that I was getting paid to go on these fabulous safaris that were equipped to give their clients the best of everything and then to be surrounded with the most beautiful exotic landscapes in the world. The game parks were still loaded with animals of every kind and we had the advantage and pleasure of just taking pictures and not disturbing them."

"A good example of how peaceful some of the days were on the tour is one time when I had landed in the Kenya game park and had taxied away from the landing strip a little way to wait for a Land Rover to pick up my passengers. We sat talking and gossiping about the day's goings on and then glancing out the window we saw there was a lion laying in the shade under the wing."

"At the famous 'Tree Top Hotel' at the foot of Mt. Kenya at night you will see a sight you will never forget. All the different kinds of animals come to drink side by side. They might be total enemies during the day and then at night drinking in common with each other. This would tell you that during the day when they are hunting for food only one is prey. It is a wonderful sight to see the gazelles and antelopes drinking along side of the lions and leopards."

"Our round robin tours made a loop and went to all the game parks. We tried to position the customers where they would have the best opportunity to photograph all the different kinds of wildlife. The area north of Nairobi had the Tree Top Hotel with the watering holes and the view of hundreds of animals. Then in the desert land there would be deer, leopards and some elephants. On the high plains we would fly over vast herds of the wildebeest, gazelles and the small foot high deer the DikDik. The guests loved flying tree top level over the lion prides lazing in the sun."

"Probably the most spectacular sight was at Lake Victoria where you could see thousands of majestic pink flamingoes standing silent as if in a painting. The multitude of water buffaloes gathered in the marshes amazed the guests with their huge size and because there were so many to see at once."

"We flew to the volcano crater in Tanzania and then on to coffee plantations near Mt. Kilimanjaro. This is where Hemmingway made his African home and did so much of his famous writing. Robert Roark lived here and wrote of his safari trips."

"I was staying in Kenya in an abandoned farm house in the high plains area which overlooks the Rift Valley and Lake Makuru. Here you will also see the pink flamingos by the thousands and thousands completely covering the lake and are a most beautiful sight. We flew and traveled in the Abadare mountains that is the last retreat of the elusive Bongo deer. These are almost extinct now because the trophy hunters went after them when tourism and hunting had become one of Africa's main industries."

"The Africans themselves are now involved in the conservation of these animals and use anti-poaching techniques to stop this slaughter. We were involved in the training of African game wardens to fly and wanted to help them in this effort. The game wardens would use a Super Cub based right at their own headquarters."

XVIII

PARTYING WITH THE ELEPHANTS

"I do remember one hair-raising event at the Samburu game lodge in northern Kenya where we were taking a group of travel agents on a tour during the rainy season. They needed to see the facilities where they would be sending their customers. These people were party animals from the word go and they had been warned so many times about the noise level of their partying every night because we were in elephant country. The elephants were used to the silence of the rainy season and would not like to be disturbed."

"This particular evening they were partying it up around midnight and the noise level inside the lodge got to such a pitch that the manager had to get on them again. I could hear the sounds of the elephants as they had moved closer to the courtyard and knew that they were disturbed. I was in my bungalow and I saw a small elephant emerge from the darkness and he came up through the little porch outside. I was afraid that the whole bungalow would be knocked down by this one elephant. But by then the whole herd of about twenty grown elephants came stampeding by the lodge and the baby elephant saw them and ran to catch up. No one was hurt and that was fortunate for us who were responsible for the tour as we tried very hard to keep the clients safe. It wasn't the elephants fault at all because they were only showing their displeasure with our intruding on their territory."

"The guests were warned to stay in their vehicles when on Safari as any of the animals could be disturbed unexpectedly by our presence. The rhino and even the wildebeests didn't like the sound of the motorized vehicles and would turn on the parked Land Rovers."

XIX

MONKEY MOVIE MAKING

"An English movie company came into the area and were going to make a children's movie about this fellow that leaves England and goes to darkest Africa. They needed to film some flying sequences and needed a pilot with a small plane and asked me to do the job. I was to fly the plane with the helmet and goggles on and the long scarf flowing out behind the plane. I thought well that is so simple."

"In the film this Englishman flies into Nairobi and sees all the buildings and tree lined boulevards and states that this is not the Africa he is looking for and needs to go further on where all the wild animals are. So then this gentleman buys a camera and a gun to protect himself and takes a suitcase full of trinkets and beads to trade with the natives. He flies out sixty miles east of Nairobi into the wilds and from the air he has spotted every kind of animal and so he lands and walks away from the airplane to take pictures of the animals."

"As the script goes on to say that the plane sits there unoccupied and a chimpanzee comes scurrying out of the brush and climbs up into the plane and spots the suitcase and opens it and throws out all the beads. Then he crawls into the pilot's seat and dons the helmet, goggles and scarf. You must know that he starts the engine with just a little trouble and slowly taxis and the little plane turns round and round in the clearing. The suspense escalates and suddenly he gives it full throttle and takes off with a burst of smoke and explosive sounds."

"We had some problems with the chimp even though he was fairly well behaved. He didn't like to throw the beads and everybody was finally showing him how and we threw beads until we were exhausted. The director said, "Oh, to hell with it and we'll just leave that part out.""

"We stopped for a late lunch and it was about three o'clock in the afternoon and it was getting hot when they started filming again. They had the chimp in the plane and the suitcase closed and was rolling the film and then the chimp calmly reached over and opened up the suitcase and flung out all the beads. Nobody said a word because they were still filming but the director waved his hand to stop because he was in stitches with laughter. We all laughed until we were sick. The filming stopped for late afternoon high tea or whatever we could find to drink and lasted until the wee hours of the morning."

"We had some more trouble with the chimp for the scenes inside the plane where they wanted to film him pressing the starter button. I had detached the starter so the engine would not run and finally I put some sticky candy on the button and he would sit there trying to get the candy and it looked like he was working hard at starting the plane."

"Now, it was my turn and I had to get suited up in this monkey suit and head gear and it was very hot and bulky. The minute I'd get it on sweat would start pouring into my eyes and I was supposed to fly that way. The last flying sequence is that the chimp would fly off and raise havoc when he flies through Nairobi dodging buildings and doing whoopty doos and the finale is the landing at the airport."

"The sweat was running into my eyes and I had a hard time judging the distance and keeping the plane flying but it's supposed to be a very bad bumpy landing anyway with a ground loop at the end. I did misjudge the distance and actually did a ground loop in order not to run off the runway into a barrier."

"With no harm done I taxied toward the hangar and a plane was coming toward me that was ready for takeoff. As the lady pilot passed me she was talking to the control tower and I heard her say, "I think there is a monkey in that airplane that just passed me!" The controller in the tower calmly replied, "Ma'm, don't you worry about it because that's just the Kenya Air Force practicing."

XX

CROP SPRAYING IN KENYA

"I went to work in Kenya for a crop spraying service and we were spraying wheat, coffee, tea and a little experimental cotton. The main crop was wheat and due to the temperature and the proximity to the equator the wheat could be grown only at high altitudes, which was about 7500 feet above sea level. Flying at this high altitude with a full load of spray was very difficult and we had other difficulties since most of the white farmers had left Kenya."

"The crew that I had working for me was an all African crew. The truck I had was a combination water truck, mixing truck and transportation for my African helpers and also carried a large tent and a cooking setup. We had two Land Rovers and I drove one and an African boy drove the other marking the fields. We had to take everything with us that we would need on the job as we would be away from the main base for long periods of time. We made quite a convoy of vehicles as we drove up into the mountains on our way to the next job."

"I was spraying with a Cessna 180 with outside spray tanks and this plane did very well at the high altitude. We were spraying wheat on the slopes of Mt. Kenya and Mt. Kilimanjaro highlands and the Thompson Falls area. These areas were very beautiful and I would never tire flying over them. It was very cold flying early in the morning because of the high altitude and there would be frost on the wings and then by ten o'clock you would have to fling off your shirt because it was so hot."

"There is much tribalism in Africa and in order for me to have a good working crew I would have to hire men from the different tribes and this would help as they would keep more or less a check on each other. I would usually have a night guard from Somalia in northern Kenya and he would not get along with any of the others but he would keep a good watch on them and what they were doing. Guns were not allowed in the camp and so the night watch carried a spear. I might find a small prey animal dead near my tent in the morning or find an intruder who had come to steal something from the farm where we were working and all of this going on not twenty feet from where I was sleeping."

"One frosty morning as I was taking off I had a collision with a Guinea fowl and broke the windshield. I happened to be wearing a white shirt and blood and guts and tissue came streaming in on me and my shirt. I managed to stop the airplane on the end of the strip and some of my loyal crew came running up and seeing all this blood on me they started screaming and wailing and they were waving their arms as they were sure I was hurt and about to die. I had a terrible time calming them down and consoling them and showing them that there was nothing wrong with me. I gathered up the feathers and explained over and over that all of this mess was from the Guinea hen. Months later I would find a feather in someone's belongings."

XXI

FERRYING PLANES ACROSS THE ATLANTIC AND ALL OVER THE WORLD

"I was working for the Piper dealer in October 1965 and my particular job was when they had sold a new plane to a customer I would accompany them on the first flight to check the motors out and to get the pilot familiar with the new airplane."

"Somehow there always seemed to be an uprising or rebel trouble wherever I happened to be at the moment. I was flying a Comanche 250 with a Rwanda registration that the Rwanda Civil aviation people wanted me to check out. Strangely enough this was the period of time that the Congo was torn by uprisings. I was spending the night in the town of Bucava at the Royal Residence Hotel. As I went to my room I was approached by several of the African servants in the hotel and they pleaded with me to let them stay in my room for a little while. I had spent time in this hotel and knew several of these boys so I let them go in and they sat huddled in a corner and I knew I would be alright, so I went to bed. I had dozed for a time and heard soft movements and sat up and looked around and there were six Africans on the floor under one little blanket. I was awakened during the night by several gun shots and the windows rattling and I just thought some of the rebel forces were having a 'shoot-em-up' good time and went back to sleep."

"About a week later I was back in Nairobi and was reading a copy of Newsweek magazine and read that the rebels had taken over the town of Bucava the night I was staying there. In November I left Nairobi and delivered an airplane, for our company, to Rhodesia and typical of my flare for finding problems, the day that I landed in Salisbury, Rhodesia was the day that Ian Smith declared independence and sealed the country off. I couldn't get out of the country and what was more incredulous I was inducted into their Air Force and within a week I was a captain in their service. By December, the situation had settled to a status quo with the British government and I asked the authorities to let me out of the service and let me go to the United States."

"I came to the United States in January and obtained my U.S. Commercial Instrument and Instructor ratings. I had been here before as a tourist but this was the first time I had been here as a resident. I decided to try out Florida as there was a lot of flying business there and I already had a contract with the Piper Company. I then picked Miami to settle into. On the 29th of January 1966 I was already hired as a ferry pilot and after being away from Africa for only a month I was on my way back to Nairobi, Kenya to deliver a Cherokee 6."

"I had never flown across the Atlantic Ocean in a single engine airplane before and was anxious as the distance was 2000 nautical miles and some of this flying would have to be during the night. That didn't bother me and was also a plus because radio reception was so much better at night. About 11:00 a.m. I took off from Ft. Lauderdale for Bermuda. I wasn't too nervous at all. Then I fueled up there and went on to Santa Maria in the Azores which was rather compelling as I didn't know how the weather would be out over the Atlantic and as things would turn out I paralleled a front for about six hours that I could have penetrated in twenty minutes. I thought it best to stay on my pre-determined course as I was flying in heavy weather all this time. This was my first experience with St. Elmo's Fire which is a fiery aura that comes off the propeller and runs along the wing to the tip. It is static electricity and is a very erie sight. The flight time took thirteen hours from Bermuda to the Azores. The next morning I flew from the Azores to Portugal."

"On the trip from Faro, Portugal eastward it was supposed to be a non-stop trip from Southern Portugal to the island of Malta in the Mediterranean Sea and I had fuel problems on that leg. I had plenty of fuel in the tanks but it would not feed properly to the engine. I made a technical landing in Tunis and I took out all of the extra gas tanks and drained them and then disassembled and checked the fuel system and found a discrepancy with the aircraft fuel selector valve. When that was finally fixed, by the next day, I went on to Malta and then on to Kartome and then from there back to Nairobi. The trip took five days and the total flying time was fifty-seven hours."

"My second trip ferrying a plane was even more interesting than the first because I didn't fly back to the United States immediately. I went from Nairobi to Leopoldville in the Congo and there I was supposed to pick up a single engine DeHavilland Otter which is a large slow airplane. The airplane was purchased by an aircraft broker in Miami and I spent three weeks getting it ready to ferry by installing extra oil and fuel tanks. I like to do all the maintenance by myself to check the engine and see that it is working well and checking the controls and the surfaces of the airplane to make sure that it is basically sound. Further preparation which takes a lot of time is studying the charts and calculating the various deviations and variations of the flight and getting with the weather people and knowing what the winds are for that period of time. You have to have a proper calibrated compass. You have to calibrate the compass before each trip as that is all you will have to guide you for long periods of time."

"I departed from Libreville, Gabon and flew to Lagos, Nigeria

Marion Reamy

and then on to Roberts Field in Monrovia and then my destination was across the South Atlantic to Natal, Brazil. But about seventeen hours later I was running short of fuel and still couldn't see the Brazilian mainland and so I took a chance and landed on the little island of Fernando de Najanja which has a landing field and a military garrison. The next day I continued on to Natal, Brazil and Belem and then flew on to the island of Antigua and then on home to Miami. The trip took a total of seventy-three hours in this large slow moving Otter which cruises roughly at 100 knots and burns maybe thirty-five gallons of fuel per hour and that shows you what a very uneconomical machine it is."

"Now, I realize that both of these first two ferry trips were strange and unusual to me and how I customarily feel about my normal flying abilities. First of all, the course across the South Atlantic is strange in itself because there are no search and rescue facilities and out there the radio is of little use and I was used to relying on my radios. There are no weather ships and therefore no weather reporting for that route and course. The radio is on VHF equipment and that could be heard only for short distances. Those first two trips were certainly trial and error and I felt I had come out of it all fairly lucky."

"My next ferry trip was in April and was delivery of another Otter to Calgary, Canada and I was looking forward to the flight as I wanted to stay awhile and visit old friends whom I hadn't seen in a few years. I made an extra trip with a little Piper Colt that I picked up in Fairbanks, Alaska and flew it to Ft. Nelson, British Columbia."

"During 1966 I spent a lot of my time flight instructing around the Miami area with an occasional ferry trip across the ocean. Of all the flying I've done I'd say the seven years that I flew the ferry pilot trips were the most enjoyable time of all of my flying experiences. I made exciting trips to many South American countries in the crop spraying airplanes and took airplanes all over the world during that time."

"During the summer of 1967 I flew in Peace River, Alberta, Canada doing forest fire back up which is not as dangerous as it

72

sounds. I flew Cessna 180's and 185's and the Cessna 170 and the Push-Pull Cubs. This was contract work for the Canadian Forestry Service and we didn't do any fire fighting and only flew the fire fighters from place to place. Most of the flying was on floats to the lakes and rivers as that is the only way to get down into that country. In September the forest fire season is over and I flew back to Miami."

"In December I was contacted about a very interesting deal where they wanted an experienced float plane pilot for a DeHavilland Beaver. I would do some support flying for a diamond company operation that was based in Georgetown, Guyana and I would be flying into the interior of Guyana. This gentleman had purchased the DeHavilland Beaver in Long Beach, California and so I went over there to pick it up and was in Yuma, Arizona on the only day that it ever snowed in Yuma. Go figure, as I can find weather where ever I fly. I flew it all the way back to Florida and then it was decided that it would be better to fly the airplane to Canada to where the floats could be purchased rather than ship them to Florida. This might sound confusing to a thinking person so I flew the plane all the way to Ontario, Canada and this is in the middle of winter, January 2nd. When I arrived in Ft. William, Ontario we installed the floats and that is some doing in the snow and cold icy weather. Our plan was to fly this airplane off this airport on the floats in the snow and then fly it all the way to Georgetown. Just clearing customs in Milwaukee, Wisconsin turned out to be a huge problem and there was too much ice near the shore of the lake to land. We couldn't land at any of the airports because of customs and after considerable radio conversations they directed us to land at a small airport that didn't have much snow. The landing was fine but then we had to truck the plane out to a small lake so that we could take off again. We finally worked our way back to Miami using the lakes we could spot."

"The flight to Guyana was almost incidental after all the nonsense of just getting back to Florida. We flew off to the Bahamas and then out to the Caribbean Islands and then to

Trinidad and on to Georgetown, Guyana. Of course the airplane didn't have Guyana registration and we tried forever to get the airplane licensed through the civil authorities there and after a month of unwanted vacation I had had it and I traveled South to Dutch Guyana."

"I took a job with the United Fruit Company and the job was flying a spray plane to control the disease on the banana crops. The only reason that they spray the bananas is that the people in the United States and other countries do not like their bananas with black spots on them. It really doesn't hurt anything as it's caused by a fungus and the spraying does get rid of that. I flew for this company about six months and then went back to the United States in October of 1968."

"In Florida I'm back in the aircraft delivery business and I'm back flying across the ocean again. Occasionally, I did some airplane repossession work and that was always interesting. I had a trip in March of 1969 when I was hired by a bank that had financed a loan on an airplane and then that party sold the plane to someone else in Puerto Rico and at that point the note defaulted. The guy in Puerto Rico knew that the plane would be picked up shortly so he left very little fuel in the tanks at the field where he had it. I arrived at the airport after dark and I decided I would check the airplane all over and found that it was low on fuel and right then mapped out my strategy and decided that I would take off before daylight the very next morning and fly to a little air strip that I had found nearby and get the fuel that I needed. In the morning I got in the plane without incident and took off with a slight grin on my face and flew on home to the States without any problems."

"I was in the delivery business again in the spring of 1969 and started to fly the Britten Norman Islanders, the twin engine fixed gear, steep take off and landing aircraft. These are popular with the smaller commuter airlines. We would fly to England and since these airplanes are fairly slow we would fly them from the factory at the Isle of White to Shannon, Ireland. There we would tank them out and then install Trans-Atlantic radio equipment.

From there we would fly them on to Reykjavik, Iceland and there we would make an overnight stop."

"This is a very nice clean town. The heating of the town is done by the geysers and springs as Iceland is situated on the crust of once active volcanoes. Then we flew on to Greenland and there is an airfield about forty miles inside the fiord, it's a little place called Narsarsuaq. The only way to fly in was to fly up the fiords as the mountains are so high on each side and the field is at the foot of a glacier. Then we were almost home with flying through Canada and on down to the United States either to New York or to Florida where the dealers were located."

"The Britten Norman Islander is a ten-place airplane with the pilot and nine passengers. We were flying with all the seats out and had installed extra gas tanks. The reason we stopped both in Greenland and Iceland was because most of the time we had head winds there and were usually battling a strong head wind. The cruising speed of the Islander was only about 125 knots and this made the flight very slow as we might have a 50 knot head wind."

"In the spring of 1969 I made an interesting trip in a Cessna 185 which I was delivering to my old stomping grounds in Somalia. Our United States Aid was giving this airplane to the Somalia Police Air Wing and I left out of Ft. Lauderdale on May 22nd. I flew from Shannon to Malta and the route that I intended to fly was from Malta to Kartome and then to Mogadisu. I left Malta and several hours later I was flying over the Libyan Desert when a radio operator in Libya advised me that the Sudan had just experienced a military takeover and all air traffic in and out of the Sudan was suspended. I took a quick look at my map and my fuel situation indicated that there was no way that I could go any way but the Sudan. I returned to Brindisi and landed and stayed overnight there. The next day checked the charts and maps and refueled and decided that I could make it to Asmara, Ethiopia. There was a problem as I would have to overfly part of the Sudan or part of Egypt and getting permission might be impossible. I took a direct flight from Brindisi to Asmara, Ethiopia with the over-flight over the Sudan and landed with very low fuel and after dark. The airport was closed and I had no flight plan. The American Embassy council had to intervene for me and I departed the next day and delivered the plane to Mogadiscio on time and as planned. On my return trip after delivering the Cessna 185 to Somalia I went to England to pick up another Britten Norman Islander for delivery in the U.S."

"With this international flying it seems all kinds of unusual things can happen and especially on the African continent. That summer was very busy for me and I had delivered five airplanes to Europe in a period of thirty days. Each trip takes thirty-five to forty-five hours so you are talking about maybe one-hundred and seventy hours I had flown in that month. Your schedule is geared to work around the weather and the main thing is to arrive at your destination at a reasonable time. You don't want to arrive at an airport at five in the afternoon, as the people receiving the plane need to inspect it. You try to set your schedule to deliver the plane early in the morning or at least by ten o'clock so that you can take your equipment out of the plane, sign the papers and catch an airliner back home all on the same day. I have trips here in my log book for example: on June 14th I flew from Boston to Gander. Then on the 15th I flew from Gander to Santa Maria and on the 16th from Santa Maria to Bordeaux, France. On the 17th I flew on to Munich Germany and on the 23rd I was already back in Wichita, Kansas picking up an airplane. This plane was going via Elmira, New York to Boston, Mass. Then I was gone again from Boston to Stevenville to Gander and across the ocean from Gander to Shannon to deliver a plane in Munich on the 28th. Then back to Norwood, Mass on the 30th and on to Boston and Gander to Shannon and delivering a plane to Dublin and then again on the 3rd of July I am back in Houston."

"Most of these trips were organized by a lady who is an expert in this business. She would have you there when you came off the airliner and all you had to do was clear customs get on the plane and be on your way."

"On August 9th I picked up a Navion from Seguin, Texas at the Navion factory there. This is in 1969 and I'm sorry to say that they are not building planes anymore. We were delivering a great number of these Navions, about one a month to Germany. It's a four place airplane and a very nice little plane."

XXII

FLYING THE GRUMMAN WIDGEON

"The company that I was working for had a Grumman Widgeon, a small amphibian built during WWII. This airplane had been modified with more powerful engines. The plane was being flown to the Congo for use in underdeveloped areas."

"I wasn't particularly fond of this airplane and had misgivings about it from the beginning. It had a pair of engines on it that I didn't like. They were radial 300 HP Lycoming and the tanking arrangements made for the extra fuel tanks that were installed had the fuel pumped up into the bottom of the main wing tanks. If by chance the lines should break I wouldn't be able to use my ferry fuel system and would also lose fuel out of the main fuel tanks. The airplanes useful load was such that there was no chance of flying the plane across the ocean non-stop and therefore you would have to fly into both Greenland and Iceland. We were doing this in the middle of October and the icing conditions in the North Atlantic were not expected to be good. The plane had no de-icing equipment and had no heaters because it had been used in a tropical climate and was going to a tropical climate."

"The trip from Ft. Lauderdale to Goose Bay, Labrador was fairly uneventful. Then I had to plan my flight from Goose Bay in such a way as to arrive in Narsarsuaq early in the day and refuel. Then I needed to have enough time to climb up across the Greenland Ice Cap, which rises to over 9,000 feet and then to continue on to Iceland. Another reason for not staying overnight in Narsarsuaq was that there were no hangar facilities and with the very low temperatures during the night these radial engines wouldn't start in the morning."

"I headed out from Goose Bay about 2:00 a.m. and flew to Narsarsuaq with very poor instrument lighting and ran into instrument weather conditions and started taking on a bit of ice. I tried to out climb the icing situation and get above the clouds but apparently too much ice had accumulated on the wings and the plane became unmanageable and I lost control. The flight characteristics of the Widgeon with ice on the wings is not very good and I ended up in a spin and a spiral dive and in the process my flashlight fell to the floor. By the time I got the airplane flying straight again by looking at the turn and bank indicators I had vertigo and didn't know if I was flying right side up or upside down. I checked the objects that I had in the cockpit to see if they were laying on the ceiling or on the floor where they belonged. After finding that I was right side up, I descended through the clouds hoping the wings would de-ice before I hit the water. I would have a real problem trying to see the water coming up in the dark and knowing that there would be icebergs out there was awful to think about. At about 400 feet above the water I came through the clouds and found that the plane was flyable. That was a relief and I continued on toward Simiutau which is a small island outside the fiord. They had a radio beacon there and with the automatic direction finder I could find my way to the beacon and it was just about daybreak as I entered the fiord. There were light snow showers but I had no problem flying up the fiord to Narsarsuaq airport."

"I refueled at the airport and after checking the weather up ahead continued on as I had another six hour flight to Reykjavik, Iceland. It was close to midnight when I landed there. The flight route from Reykjavik to Shannon and then on to Spain and Casablanca and then on to Los Palmas was uneventful. When I landed at Dakar the tail wheel parted company with the airplane and ground off a little piece of the keel. The mechanics there at Roberts Field repaired it and I flew on to Libreville, Gabon. My intention was to stay over at Libreville and then go on the next day to Kinshasia (the new name for Leopoldville) which is in the Congo. However, the people of Libreville would not let me stay there because of political problems in the country. They were running guns at that time for the rebel factions in the Biafra war effort and they wanted me to leave as soon as possible for Kinshasia, Zaire. It was several hours after dark when I landed at Kinshasia and as my flight plan did not call for me to land on Sunday night they immediately threw me in jail. After doing such a friendly act for them by flying all this way to bring them the plane they put me in jail!"

"It took two days for the people who were supposed to come and get the airplane to finally find it sitting on the ramp at the airport and then to start wondering where the pilot was. Then they finally came to get me out of jail."

"They have a jail system there that really works for them. They think that only criminals are in jail and they think that the good people who are not in jail should not have to feed criminals. So they don't feed them or supply them with anything. Their families have to bring them food and whatever they might need. The real criminals that were caught were treated harshly. The prisoner that is a pickpocket would have his hand cut off or people caught in adultery would have a brand put on their forehead that would be there forever."

"This is a male dominated society and adultery is just not permitted. The young women are forced into a ceremony where usually some older woman in the house actually sew up the female sex part and thereafter the woman can't have children or can't enjoy the sex act. The male is everything here and the women spend all of their time with the little boy babies and ignore every need of the girl babies. The women are virtual slaves in some of these countries and are only baby makers."

"Getting back to the flying, we were also delivering small airplanes to be used for agricultural purposes in South America. We delivered everything from Piper Pawnees to AeroCommander spray planes and took them anywhere in South America."

"We flew a route contrary to the route most pilots would fly where they would follow a course either on the East coast or the West coastline to Argentina. We would leave Ft. Lauderdale and land in Jamaica and continue on to Barranquilla, Columbia and then go direct to Leticia, Columbia. Then I would fly right across the middle of the Amazon jungle and cross the Amazon River at that point and then on to Trinidad, Bolivia, to Santa Cruz, to Buenos Aires, Argentina. We cut off 1,000 miles by doing this and cut the cost way down. We are in an airplane without any radio aides and no instruments for flying under instrument weather conditions."

"I took a delivery to Bucaramango, Columbia in February 1970 in an Aero Commander from Albany, Georgia where the airplane was built. The flight from Georgia to Ft. Lauderdale to Cartagena, Columbia is a one day trip and then from there to Barranquilla and on to Bucaramango is about three hours and forty minutes and is spent mainly trying to get over the mountains. All of this flying amounts to about eighteen hours and twenty minutes. The reason that you can fly for such a long time in these agricultural airplanes is because we use the hopper for fuel. Since these were new planes we would fill the hopper with gasoline and hook it up as an additional gas tank. These are small airplanes and with an additional two-hundred gallons of fuel and a fuel consumption of twelve gallons per hour you would have enough for the long runs. The fuel would last longer than your mind and you were not real sharp after ten hours. The total trip from Ft. Lauderdale to Buenos Aires was about fifty-seven hours with the stops."

XXIII

NEVER FLY A SUDDEN
STOP ENGINE

"I was called upon to ferry a couple of Ag Cats to Costa Rica and had to pick up the plane at the factory in Georgia. The second plane was to be flown by a factory pilot. It was terrible weather when we arrived at the factory and we were told to wait and they would bring the planes around to us. As they were taxiing the planes, one nosed up in the mud and took a sudden stop on the engine. They pulled the prop off the plane and put a new prop on it and asked me to fly that one. I told them no way that I would fly that plane unless they put a new engine in it. The pilot from the factory insisted that there was nothing wrong with the engine or the prop and he ran the engine up to show me. I too was determined and told him, "Fine, then you fly the plane."

"Our route was down through Florida and out over the water to Costa Rica and the only navigational aide we had with us was the magnetic compass. When we reached the coast of Costa Rica we were about sixty miles off course which wasn't too bad. The trees are right down to the edge of the water on the coast and the surf breaks right up into the trees."

"As we approached the coast line I noticed the other plane starting to descend and I dropped back to see what he was doing and as I drew alongside of him I noticed that there was no prop on his plane and realized the crank shaft had been cracked in the nose up accident at the airport and now it had just sheared off. As we passed along the coast which had very dense jungle right at the water's edge we began searching frantically for a place for him to put his plane down. We had no radio equipment to request help from someone but we did find a small clearing in the jungle just about big enough to fit his plane into. He couldn't land there but would have to pancake in."

"He circled over the spot and finally stalled the plane right over the spot and crashed the plane into the opening. I felt certain that he was surely killed in the crash and I slowly circled the site and was so happy to see him come crawling out of the wreck and he signaled to me that he was ok."

"I hated to leave him but had to fly on to my destination and when I arrived I reported the crash to the local authorities and they seemed to take it seriously and I left feeling that they would take care of getting the pilot to safety."

"Two weeks later when I finally got back to Georgia the first thing I did was get to a phone to call the pilot's wife to see how he was and to see how it all worked out. When she answered the phone and I asked about him she said that she thought that he was with me. I was astounded and could hardly ask her if she had been told that her husband had crashed in the jungle. She was crying and I felt just terrible that I hadn't checked back to see if they had found him. I immediately got hold of the Coast Guard and found that it hadn't been reported to them. This was all so crazy and yet I felt that even though a lot of time had passed he probably was still ok and that gave me hope. The Coast Guard contacted the authorities in Costa Rica and they hadn't even bothered to go and look for him. So the Coast Guard sent out a search plane and I went along as I knew the spot where he had gone down. It didn't take much flying along the coast until I spotted the opening where he had crashed but every speck of the airplane had been carted off by the locals and the pilot was nowhere to be found. As it turned out the local guerrillas had found him and taken him prisoner and they were holding him for $1,500 ransom. Incredulous! While they had him prisoner they had carted him all over the Costa Rican jungle on the back of a burro which aggravated a back injury he had received in the crash. The American Embassy ransomed him from these local outlaws and he finally got back to the states. When I met up with him again I couldn't help myself and told him, "I told you so!" "Never fly a sudden stopped engine." Over that carelessness they lost a whole airplane and injured the pilot."

XXIV

FERRYING PLANES IS WHAT I DO

"It was the summer of 1970 and I noticed a Piper Navajo going to Undola Kiffly in Rhodesia. This is about 1000 miles South of Nairobi, Kenya and so I ferried the plane there and two days later I'm back in Bainbridge, England on the Isle of Wright picking up a Britton-Norman Islander and so I ferried that to the Azores and then back to Gander."

"The Britton-Norman Islander's were built in Britain and we would pick them up there and then take them back to the United States. Commuter airlines in the United States were snapping them up as fast as we could get them here. The East coast airlines and flight services in the Caribbean were all eager to buy them and they were sold all over the place and even as far away as Texas. They are like a taxi cab and hold ten people with five rows of seats, side by side. They were a very popular economical money maker."

"I had another very interesting trip on July 26th when I was supposed to fly a Grumman Widgeon back to the United States for maintenance and overhaul. This plane had lived its life and done its work in Nigeria, Africa and a pilot had flown it as far as Shannon, Ireland and I had the contract to fly it back to the United States. The problem was that I had tried to pick up this plane once before and it had caught fire on me shortly after takeoff from Shannon but I had managed to make it back to the airport. This time I decided that with a plane I didn't quite trust I would fly over as much land mass as I could so I flew to Belfast, Ireland and on to Stornoway, Scotland and on to the northern point of Scotland and then went on to Reykjavik, Iceland. I knew I couldn't make it to the West coast of Nassusua and had to land at a little airport on the East coast of Greenland called Koolsook. The only reason it's here is support of a radar station that is manned by the Danish Air Force personal. From there I flew to Nassuak and then on to Goose Bay and then to Gander, Newfoundland and Malta and then to Fulton, Maine and cleared customs there and then down to Franklin, Virginia. Then I flew out to Hilton Head, South Carolina and on to Miami. All that summer I was back and forth to England picking up the Britain Norman Islanders."

"In October another pilot and I started a very interesting delivery trip taking two Britain Norman Islanders to a commuter airline in Tahiti. I had not spent much time flying in the Pacific and since the airplanes did not have the fuel capacity to fly from the west coast of the U.S. to Hawaii we determined that we'd fly the planes on the eastern route to England and then on to Paris. We were flying for a French company and they wanted some publicity pictures for Air Tahiti Airlines. We flew from Paris to Malta and on to Ankara, Turkey, to Tehran, Iran and on to ShaSha and from there we went across the Indian Ocean to Bombay, India and across India to Maddras, India. From there we flew to Kuala-Lampur in Malaysia then to Bali. This is the island with the beautiful women and the beautiful scenery so we landed there to look at the scenery. The next day we pushed on to Cumbali, Indonesia and to the North shores of Australia at Darwin we continued on to Port Moresby, New Guinea and then on to Henderson Field and landed at the airport on the island. From that field we took off for Nandy and from there to the island of American Samoa, Pango Pango and then to Tahiti. We stayed overnight in Tahiti and then took an airliner back home the next day. Tahiti was already a sophisticated tourist spot as the French were running it."

"It was the middle of December and I was delivering a Britain Norman Islander to Ottawa, Canada and I had made so many trips that winter that it became a natural thing to fly in the ice and snow. But this trip suddenly took a turn for the worse as I had about three inches of ice accumulated on the windshield and all over the plane. I couldn't see the runway as I came near the airport and thought I might just have to drop it down somewhere. But the radar controller came to my rescue by bringing me into the runway at an angle and I opened the side window so that I could see the runway. I was really proud of that airplane for holding together with the weight of all of that ice on it and simply proved what a good winter flying airplane it was. A happy note here is that I got to be home for Christmas and New Years that year due to the weather."

"My log books show that I flew one hundred and eighty trips across the Atlantic Ocean."

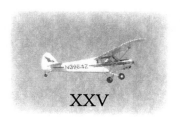

XXV

PERSUADING RUTH

"That same year I met a beautiful girl who was a secretary for the flying service where I worked and over time I persuaded her to marry me. I told Ruth that I would give her everything that she ever dreamed of having and a lot more, especially trips in my airplane. We were married in 1972. I wanted to spend more time with Ruth and wanted to stay put for awhile so I quit the ferrying business."

XXVI

ASHES TO ASHES

"I was in the Miami area when I got a call from a funeral director asking me if I could handle a flight for him where one of his clients had requested that the cremated ashes of their loved one be flown out over the Gulf of Mexico and spread across the sea. I told him that I could accommodate him and a few days later he called and asked if it was a good day to spread the ashes and I said that we were ready to go."

"I prepared a Cessna to make the flight out there and the funeral director handed me the little cremation box which was about the size of a cigar box. Then he told me that he had no intention of flying out over the Gulf with me. One of the mechanics in the shop decided that he wanted to go with me. I knew that the guy was slightly superstitious and squeamish and warned him that when it came time to put the ashes out of the plane he was to open the door and hold it open with his foot. Then he had to carefully open the box and hold it as close to the open door as he could get it and then hopefully the suction of the air would draw the ashes out. He wasn't that fond of flying and he didn't think that opening the door and holding it open with his foot was a very good idea. He had a better idea of how it should be done. He thought that my idea wasn't safe with the door open and he decided that he would do it like it is done in aerial photography. He would open the window!"

"It was a gorgeous day as we flew out over the Gulf. There was a blue sky and blue water with a few puffy clouds overhead. The mechanic opened the window and as he lifted the box to pour out the ashes they blew right back into the cockpit. The ashes whirled around and around and they were on the dash and stuck to the windshield and stuck to the headliner. They were on the hat shelf and all over us and worst of all they got in our eyes. The guy was horrified and he was trying to talk with ashes in his mouth and I just had to hold myself together and fly the plane."

"When we got back to the airport he was sick and ran to his car and took off. I took the vacuum cleaner out to the plane and cleaned it all up and figured that was the least I could do."

"The next morning the mechanic showed up for work and somebody made a remark about the ashes and he got upset all over again and told us, "If anybody makes one more remark I'm going home." Nobody said a word until coffee break about 11:00 and the owner of the shop and the rest of the crew were sitting around drinking coffee. When the mechanic walked in the owner kicked the vacuum cleaner and said, "Well, how do you like it in there?" He did this several times and finally the mechanic said, "Fred, what are you doing?" and Fred replied, "Well, I'm just trying to find out if this guy you were trying to throw out of the airplane yesterday likes it here in this vacuum cleaner bag!" We didn't see that fellow again for two whole days and I felt really bad because it could have been my fault and then again maybe not."

"I've had some of the strangest requests from people that want ashes thrown out of an airplane. This one request in particular came from a funeral director and he told me that his client had been a yacht captain and had stated in his will that he wanted his ashes spread out at sea in a very precise location. I told him that I would do it and looked at the map and this place was 500 miles from Miami. It was way down the island chain and probably half way between Cacaus and the Turk Islands. I figured out how many flying hours flying time it would be down there and he said, "OK" and said that he would have to go over the estimate with the family and get back to me. A few days later he contacted me and said the family agreed to the cost and he brought out the ashes and I set out on the trip."

"I planned on going to Nassau to refuel and then fly out to that particular spot that the captain had requested. I flew out over the open water going to Nassau and when I lost sight of land and was flying along I said to myself, "This is the craziest thing in the world to do." I figured that the captain would agree with me that the best idea was to fly thirty miles out to sea and spread the ashes and then fly on to Bimini and have a good day lying on the beach."

"Since we're on these kinds of stories I'll tell you about the day I got a call to pick up a person on an island south of Cuba, Grande Camon Island. I had word that someone was seriously ill there and needed to be brought out. I flew down there in a Cherokee 6 with a stretcher and they loaded the man on board. He was not coherent and his skin color was very, very poor. I had my doubts that he could even make the trip back to Florida. That is just what happened and by the time we hit Key West I tried to find a pulse and couldn't find any."

"What happened next is very unusual. The man was fairly tall and his legs were sticking out about six inches beyond the stretcher and during the flight his feet had become lodged behind the rudder pedals. I hadn't used the rudder pedals much during the flight and I didn't know rigor mortis had set in. His body had stiffened up a little and when I landed in Miami I couldn't get him out."

"I had called ahead for a doctor and they made arrangements for an ambulance to be there but I wanted a doctor to verify that the man was dead. There was a little vacant period there as the ambulance didn't want to take him and they had already verified that he was dead and we were waiting for the funeral people. I wanted to get the body out of the plane and the only person I could see in the customs area of the general aviation department was an airport employee and I asked him to please come and help me."

"The body was very stiff and with the feet stuck behind the pedals I needed somebody to kind of bend the body, so to speak. So I was in the plane struggling to release the man's feet from the pedals and this fellow was holding the man by the torso trying to pull him out the door. My helper must have been superstitious because he was not doing too well with the corpse and all of a sudden while he was bending the body, some of the body gasses escaped and made a huge burping sound. The last I saw of the guy he was falling off the wing backwards and then he disappeared going around the hanger. I just had to wait there until the funeral people came to help me untangle this man from my airplane."

"These stories remind me of something strange that happened to me years ago. I had just met a very good looking girl that someone had introduced me to. I took her out to dinner and we had a few drinks and then I took her home and she invited me in for a drink. I sat down on the couch and as she was pouring the drinks, she said, "Will you pardon me while I give my guy in the closet a drink?" I had visions of this big guy in the closet coming out and beating the hell out of me. She went to the closet and brought out this urn and set it down and opened the lid and poured in the Scotch. She explained that these ashes were from her deceased husband and that he liked Scotch. I didn't date her again."

XXVII

LENETTE, ALABAMA 1973

"On this occasion a fellow living in Iowa bought a Navion in Florida and he contacted me to fly it up there. I decided to take Ruth along and make it a little vacation for us. I planned to fly the trip in one day but then we ran into some bad weather and had to try for a landing in the little town of Lenette, Alabama. The airport lies in a valley along the river and I managed to squeeze in there in spite of the low visibility. By that time the weather was so bad that we weren't going anyplace anyway."

"The next morning the weather still hadn't cleared and we were waiting around when the fellow who owned the airport said he wanted to show me some of the projects he was working on. He was metalizing the wings of Piper Tri-Pacers and modifying the wings by lengthening them to increase the span and improve the performance. Another project he was into was putting nose wheels on a Stinson, which is normally a tail wheel airplane. There were three of them sitting on the field and it looked like he had done a very nice job carrying out the modification."

"The day wore on and we had talked and talked and I told him that I was an aeronautical engineer and then he took me to his pet project. It was a flying saucer! He had been building on this flying saucer since the early 50's. It was built inside this huge hangar and it was shaped exactly like a saucer and the size of this dish was approximately 33 feet in diameter by 36 feet high. It was powered by two 85 HP Continental engines. It had a two-place cockpit sticking up out of the top made of tubing and I suppose would eventually be fabric covered. I've not heard a thing about this strange craft since I was there and had always wanted to get back up there to see what he'd done with it but never had the opportunity."

XXVIII

AN OTTER MINUS A TAIL WHEEL

"In the early seventies a fellow in Miami had rebuilt a single engine Otter and wanted me to test fly it. During the test I found out that the engine seemed to be running lean and every time that I tried to change the mixture the engine would start to cut out. I didn't know exactly what was wrong with it so I was going through all sorts of things that I could think of and then I decided that it was the carburetor. I told them that the carburetor seemed to be running excessively lean because the minute you touched it, it would start to cut out."

"Someone had already purchased the airplane and they wanted me to check the new owner out. Jack, the new owner, was getting pushed for time and so he asked me if I would be willing to fly him to Alaska instead of just taking these check rides. So again, I decided to make a vacation of it for Ruth and I. Jack brought his girlfriend along and so I loaded everybody into the plane. I didn't know that Jack's wife was up in the Aleutian Islands in Alaska working her fingers to the bone keeping their hunting lodge open, while he took his girl friend to Florida."

"Anyway, we took off from Miami, but then about every

twenty or thirty miles the engine would cut out or hesitate a fraction of a second and then go on again. I played around with the mixture and the carburetor heat and the engine would smooth right out and I would relax for a minute. This particular engine sounds kind of strange anyway. It is a 9-cylinder radial engine with a geared propeller, augmenter tubes and the noise inside the plane is deafening and it is virtually impossible to talk to each other during the flight."

"We stopped for fuel at Waltersboro, South Carolina and the weather was getting lousy but I decided to take off anyway. During the subsequent take-off the engine signed off, it just you know quit!"

"It was popping, banging and backfiring and all that kind of stuff and here I had this heavily loaded airplane with three passengers. Jack insisted that we take all kinds of spare parts with us for his use in Alaska; engine parts, propeller parts, hydraulic wheel skis and our luggage and I could just imagine all of that stuff coming loose and heck it was loose and what I could imagine was it all flying around the cabin if we crashed."

"It was kind of frightening to look out of the windshield and see only trees in front of us. I was sitting in the left seat and Jack is in the right seat and he's supposed to be this 4,000 hour experienced pilot. When this thing started popping and hiccupping Jack's hands flew clear off the controls and it was all mine. I started turning the plane around, trying to get back to the airport. I was working everything and he was no help. I kept lowering the nose of the plane to see if there was a place to land and I already know there was no place because all I've seen is this narrow road and I know the wings will be clipped off as there are obstructions along the road. When I finally suck it around the airplane is already so slow, I'm behind the power curve altogether and the plane just whacks right on down, stalls on me and goes in. It hits so hard that the gear spreads to the point that the prop hits the ground and this is on a tail dragger airplane."

"I had managed to get the plane over the fence and onto the grass at the airport. The engine would idle so I taxied back to the hangers. Jack and I couldn't find anything wrong with the plane from the hard landing and he thinks that's all there is going to be to it. Then he asks me to test fly the airplane! I was incredulous at his even asking me to do it. I told him, "No way, unless you go up with me." So we get into the airplane and taxi out to the end of the runway, run it up and everything seems to be all right. We take off and the minute the tail wheel lifts off the ground the plane starts to act strangely. The airplane is flying but the engine starts to act up and then we see this car on the ground below us and the car is running up and down the runway like crazy. A guy is hanging out of the window and is trying to show us something!"

"Then I see what he is holding! It's the electric steerable tail wheel that has dropped out of our airplane! The whole mechanism has just fallen right out. The whole thing! This is a big unit with a big vertical shaft and the whole assembly has just fallen out and I didn't even know it."

"I look at Jack and tell him, "This is it. I'm going to land this so and so before something else falls off this stupid airplane!" When we hit the ground, we were skidding and there is this horrible grinding sound as the plane skids around with no tail wheel. When we've stopped we bail out before the whole thing blows up!"

"The fellow that runs the airport is also a milkman and has these large milk cartons and we use them to jack the tail of the airplane up until we have it high enough to get the tail wheel shoved back in. I taxied it over and parked it and we never got back in it again."

"I did take one of the manifold pipes off the engine and it was absolutely loaded with oil and the impeller section was gone and it was shot. It would have been a heck of a lot cheaper to find out that there was something wrong with the engine in Miami than to find out about it almost six-hundred miles away and then to put our lives at risk to boot."

EPILOGUE

The Memorial Service for Hans Vandervlugt was held at the beautiful Episcopal Church of the Good Shepherd in Corpus Christi, Texas. Over five-hundred people attended the service to bid farewell to Hans. His wife, Ruth, and his sons, close friends, customers, businessmen and students that he had taught to fly were all there. The students had come from Holland, England, Africa, and Canada and from all across the country to show their love and respect for Hans.

Many came to the service because they had known Hans for so many years and thought of him as a dear friend. Most everyone thought he was the best pilot in South Texas. Hans will live on in the memory of all who knew and loved him. If Hans could have had a moment before his leaving these might have been the words he would have left with us.

I'd like the memory of me
To be a happy one.
I'd like to leave an after glow
Of smiles when life is done.
I'd like the tears of those who
Weep to dry before the sun.
Of happy memories that I leave
When life is done.

unknown

CPSIA information can be obtained at www.ICGtesting.com
Printed in the USA
LVOW052250191212

312491LV00001B/39/P